FROM WORD TO IMAGE

THE TOBIN WING

1984

Marion Koogler McNay Art Museum
San Antonio, Texas

Published through the courtesy of the Tobin Foundation, San Antonio, Texas.
Copyright 1984 Marion Koogler McNay Art Museum
ISBN 0-916677-02-8 All rights reserved.
Library of Congress Catalog Card No.: 84-62125
Printed in the United States of America.

INTRODUCTION

The exhibition "From Word to Image", and its accompanying catalog, are designed to acquaint further the scholarly community and the visiting public with the variety of treasures that constitute the Tobin Library. Exhibitions have been planned for the next five years with the same intent. Some exhibitions will be devoted to single artists, such as Gontcharova, or families of artists, like the Bibiena. Others will scan the entire holdings. Without a catalog, these continuing exhibitions would provide us only with lists of titles; instead we want them to emphasize the strong individuality that marks the Tobin Library.

A great library, like a collection of paintings, may be considered from many points of view. Since the Tobin Library has a very personal orientation, it is pertinent to have the collector himself lead us through the imaginative threads that bind it into a whole.

John Palmer Leeper
Director

FROM WORD TO IMAGE

1. Giacomo Torelli. *The Cave of the Winds.* Engraving. Scene design for Act I, scene 2 of *Il Bellerofonte.*

"From Word to Image" connotes a firm commitment to the concept of the validity of a visual response to the stimulus of a text, whether this be a theatrical production, a cinematographic exercise or a typographic answer to the challenge of the dramatic text. A text thus inspires creative expression.

From the earliest *livres des fête* through their direct lineal descendants, the word was celebrated. From these words came the visual realizations in costume and scenic investiture. When they are co-mingled, they form the backbone (or in bibliographic terms: the spine) of this library. This exhibition will explore several manifestations: the illustrated text as a record of a specific event; secondly the beautiful book created for the sake of its own artistic validity where the illustrations are an art unto themselves and, finally, costume and stage designs based on plays (or librettos) quite divorced from the text itself and used for their intended purpose, as guides for costumes and scenographers.

In this journey of exploration of the library, let us remember that although the waters are fairly well charted, they are often filled with icebergs and that the mass of material that supports these visible manifestations lies beneath in both a literal and figurative sense. We have sought but examples, not a complete bibliography of the holdings which would soon be out of date. Such is the way of a growing collection.

The *fête* books constituted, very early, the conception of the original library. Not only did they support research in theater design, but also in architecture; not only in costume but also in choreography, sometimes even of horses. (The early "horse operas" were invaluable excuses for the ostentation and display of the earliest theatrical spectacles.)

These volumes, often of surpassing grandeur, served many purposes: they chronicled an event, they offered indisputable evidence of the intentions of the patron and provided convenient opportunities to apprise the outside world of the prodigious wealth, taste, discrimination and determination to out-display rival courts whose magnificence would be sorely taxed to match the "splendure, grandure and allure" of the event described. Although we limit ourselves to dramatic presentations with a known text, there were similar volumes dealing with births, weddings, royal entries into cities, royal progresses, triumphal arches, pyrotechnical extravaganzas, stately catafalques for funereal functions, fabulous feasts (replete with canines gobbling up left-overs) mountains of spun sugar for the proletariat, armadas of lanterns, avenues of torches; the list is as fanciful and fantastic as the urge to display was uninhibited.

As the dramatic event was integral to these celebrations, it is obvious that its delineation was essential. It is to be remembered too that single point perspective (which will be the subject of a later exhibition) is from a fixed point in the theater: the place occupied by the ruling prince who made these excursions into the improbable not only possible but practical.

We have selected a series of examples generally from the third quarter of the seventeenth century. The Torelli, representing the master at his most inventive, is mirrored by the 1668 Burnacini which is perhaps the most authoritative report of an event for a variety of reasons. (*Il Pomo D' Oro* was originally scheduled to coincide with the celebration of the marriage of Leopold I and Margherita of Spain in December 1666 but had to be postponed several times due to fire, snow and illness.) *Il Pomo D' Oro* finally opened two

2. Ludovico Burnacini. *Toppling of the Tower by Jupiter.* Engraving. Scene design for Act V, scene 9 of *Il Pomo D'Oro.*

3. André Derain. *Herodias*. Watercolor, gouache and ink. Illustration for *Salomé*.

years later, its twenty-three sumptuous settings having required the construction of a theater. The wedding festivities included one of the aforementioned horse operas. Burnacini also contributed the decor for *Il Fuoco Eterno Custodito delle Vestale* which translates exactly as one thinks it does and the leading character is, not surprisingly, Claudia. In the penultimate scene, Apollo makes his heavenward departure after rekindling the eternal fire but he does receive a little assistance as is evidenced by the magnifying glasses included in the illustration.

Gods and machines kept things going in the Baroque opera. Not so in the nineteenth century as we *segue* (quite improbably) to the *Salomé* of Oscar Wilde, which gives us the opportunity to examine two contrasting approaches to the luxuriant text. The Limited Editions Club sought to recapture one of the publishing events of the nineteenth century, the Aubrey Beardsley illustrated play, of verbal richness verging on the grotesque, with all its eroticism and self-centered depravity. In contrast, in the same slip case, the publishers chose one of the leading artists of his day, André Derain, to attack again the problems presented by the play. The illustrations were

printed on black paper by the pochoir process. We are exhibiting the original drawings in their freshness of approach, often verging on the hilarious as in the quite complacent Iokanaan and the even more unconcerned Herodias with her classic gesture familiar to those who travel the borscht circuit. The four Jews have never been captured more stylishly and the heroine (?) herself in her determined sexuality.

The suite of lithographs by Eugéne Delacroix are often considered monuments of the illustrator's art. Showing them in juxtaposition with a contemporary trade edition is no accident. They were meant to "illustrate" and that they do, in a curiously detached way. There is little of the immediacy of the great Delacroix prints: there is even a certain awkwardness about them.

Another approach to the same play, that of consciously producing the beautiful book for the sake of its own being, is exemplified in the Cranach *Hamlet* and the examples from small presses, notably the Grabhorn Press in California, whose annual publication of a Shakespeare play was an eagerly awaited event in the book world.

Complimenting the Cranach *Hamlet* with its great

woodcuts by Craig are two sketches for the play by the artist. One gives an uncanny sense of the towering spaces envisioned by the artist (who had to add paper to fulfill the concept). The other is a double-sided page full of the dramatic excitement of the battle scene. The tranquility of the woodcuts is brought to powerful life in his attempt to capture the moment of action.

Complimenting the small press editions of the Shakespeare plays are costume designs for several of the celebrated Canadian Stratford productions notably by Tanya Moiseiwitsch. In Shakespeare, the text itself is quite often design enough for the scenery, witness the passage from *Henry V*:

O! for a Muse of fire,
  that would ascend
The brightest heaven of
  invention;
A kingdom for a stage,
  princes to act
And monarchs to behold
  the swelling scene.
      Prologue
      *The Life of Henry
      the Fifth*

The rather improbable *Der Rosenkavalier* is a charming volume about which little is known. The Hoffmannsthal text is illustrated and hand-lettered by Rafaello Busoni, the

4. Eugène Delacroix. *This skull, Sir, was that of Yorrick, the King's jester . . . alas, poor Yorrick.* Lithograph. Illustration for Act V, scene 1 of *Hamlet*.

5. Edward Gordon Craig. *Hamlet Decor.* Watercolor.

6. Rafaello Busoni. *Act III*.   Watercolor. Illustration for *Der Rosenkavalier*.

son of the celebrated composer. Bound in vellum, it is a presentation object from Berlin in 1939. The tiny maquette from Sarah Caldwell's production is by Helen Pond and Herbert Senn.

The art of the cinema has been a unique manifestation of the twentieth century. The recent celebration of the influence of Jean Cocteau in so many areas of literature and the film are easily mirrored in the sumptuous edition of *L'Eternal Retour.* The text is complete as are some directions: what is important are the astonishing photographs that capture the essence of the work. The book is complimented by Cocteau's portrait of Jean Marais, the leading actor in so many Cocteau productions.

The complete suite of drawings by Robert Israel for *Akhnaton,* Philip Glass' latest opera, represents the artist's second excursion into the mysterious world created by Glass, whose *Satyagraha* received acclaim throughout the world. The exhibition of the designs for *Akhnaton* in San Antonio coincides with the Houston Grand Opera's 1984 production, which will be its American premier. Israel has exemplified the return of the artist to the theater and his unique insight into the texts involved seem to epitomize the concept of drama inspiring the creative image.

The *Orfeo* of Gluck might appear to have been written with Louise Nevelson in mind. The publication came about as a result of the opening of the Tobin Library. Bill Katz, a collaborator on the publication, attended the opening and, inspired by the grandeur of the *livres des fêtes* in the collection, designed a more contemporary version of the festival book. Various objects relating to the production are exhibited, as well as working proofs for the first night libretto and the forthcoming publication.

• • •

Requiem for the Met. #2 is included in the exhibition and used on the catalog cover for a variety of reasons. The most obvious is that I admire George L. K. Morris and the somewhat forgotten painters he represents. With its representation of the score of *Der Rosenkavalier* in the left hand corner, it would also seem to exemplify the thematic reason for the show. Most important: I like the picture.

There is a nostalgic set of coincidences that were unknown to Morris. My first opera at the Metropolitan Opera in its Broadway home was on a snow driven afternoon. We had queued for hours until we spotted a small sign saying "Opera Tickets" and made our way around the corner to pay fifty dollars for T1 and T3. It was Ljuba Weltisch's first live broadcast of *Salomé* and my birthday. The experience was as unforgettable as the gold leaf and faded crimson brocade of the old Sherry Restaurant, presided over by the towering portraits of the great singers of the past, canvases that have been discreetly herded into "Founders' Hall" in the opera house now in Lincoln Center.

Morris painted two pictures in homage to destroyed landmarks, the other an homage to Penn Station. As a final irony, the Metropolitan picture found a temporary home in "Founders' Hall" during the Centennial Celebration, replacing one of the divas that had escaped the corral.

Robert L. B. Tobin

DETAILS

HEADDRESS, NECKLACE, BEADS

GOWN

7. Robert Israel. *Nefertiti in Coronation Gown.* Watercolor and felt-tip pen. Costume design for *Akhnaton.*

8. Ludovico Burnacini. *The Athenians Preparing to Make War on Troy.* Engraving. Scene design for Act II, scene 10 of *Il Pomo D'Oro.*

9. Giacomo Torelli. *Harbor in Patera*. Engraving. Scene design for the Prologue of *Il Bellerofonte*.

10. Eugène Delacroix. *. . . her garments, heavy with their drink, pulled the poor wretch . . .* Lithograph. Illustration from
Act IV, scene 7 of *Hamlet*.

11. André Derain. *Iokanaan, the Prophet*. Watercolor, gouache and ink. Illustration for *Salom*é.

12. Rafaello Busoni. *Act II.* Watercolor. Illustration for *Der Rosenkavalier.*

13. Robert Israel. *Ram/Khnum and Hawk/Horus Gods - Four Canopic Jars*. Watercolor and
felt-tip pen. Costume design for *Akhnaton*.

CATALOG OF THE EXHIBITION

Note: Catalog entries are in chronological order according to medium.

BOOKS

Terentius Afer, Publius. *Comoedieae Cum Directorio Glosa Interlineali, et Commentariis Donato, Guidone, Ascensio* (The Commentary of Donatus on Terence). Published with woodcuts in Strassburg, 1496.

Procaccino, Carlo Antonio, Illustrator. *L'Adamo,* by Giovanni Battista Andreini. Published in Milan, 1617.

Torelli, Giacomo, Designer. *Il Bellerofonte,* by Vicenzo Nolfi. Published in Venice, 1642. **Illustrated on pages 6 and 17.**

Burnacini, Giovanni, Designer. *La Gara,* by Alberto Vimina. Published in Vienna, 1652.

Tacca, Ferdinando, Designer. *Ercole in Tebe,* by G. A. Moniglia. Published in Florence, 1661. Plates engraved by Valerio Spada.

Tacca, Ferdinando, Designer. *Il Mondo Festeggiante,* attributed to Alessandro Carducci. Published in Florence, 1661. Plates engraved by Stefano della Bella.

Santurini, Francesco, Designer. *Fedra Incoronata,* by Pietro Paolo Bissari. Published in Monaco, 1662. Plates engraved by Matthias Küsel.

Burnacini, Ludovico, Designer. *Sieg-streit der Lufft und Wassers,* by Francesco Sbarra. Published in Vienna, 1667.

Burnacini, Ludovico, Designer. *Il Pomo d'Oro,* by Francesco Sbarra. Published in Vienna, 1668. Plates engraved by M. Küssel. **Illustrated on pages 8 and 16.**

Burnacini, Ludovico, Designer. *Il Fuoco Eterno Custodito delle Vestale,* by Antonio Draghi. Published in Vienna, 1674. Plates engraved by M. Küsel.

Bibiena, Ferdinando and Francesco, Designers. *L' Eta del Oro,* by Lotto Lotti. Published in Piacenza, 1690. Plates engraved by Martial Dubois and Carlo Antonio Forti.

Bibiena, Ferdinando and Francesco, Designers. *L' Idea di Tutte le Perfezione,* by Lotto Lotti. Published in Piacenza, 1690. Plates engraved by Martial Dubois and Carlo Antonio Forti.

Michetti, Niccolo, Designer. *Carlo Magno,* by Cardinal Ottoboni. Published in Rome, 1729.

Bibiena, Giancarlo, Designer. *Alessandro nell'Indie,* by Pietro Metastasio. Published in Lisbon, 1755.

Craig, Edward Gordon. *On the Art of the Theatre.* Published in Chicago, 1911.

Craig, Edward Gordon. *De L' Art du Theatre.* Published in Paris, 1912.

Delacroix, Eugène, Illustrator. *Hamlet,* by William Shakespeare. Published in Leipzig, 1913.

Nowak, Willi, Illustrator. *Ariadne auf Naxos,* by Hugo Hoffmannsthal. Published in Munich, 1922.

Craig, Edward Gordon, Illustrator. *The Tragedie of Hamlet,* by William Shakespeare. Published in Weimar by Cranach Press, 1930.

Busoni, Rafaello, Illustrator. *Der Rosenkavalier,* by Hugo Hoffmannsthal. Original watercolors and hand lettering completed in Berlin, 1933. **Illustrated on pages 13 and 20.**

Beardsley, Aubrey, Illustrator. *Salomé,* by Oscar Wilde. Published by The Limited Editions Club, London, 1938.

Derain, André, Illustrator. *Salomé,* by Oscar Wilde. Published by The Limited Editions Club, London, 1938.

Cocteau, Jean. *L' Eternal Retour.* Published in Paris, 1947.

Grabhorn, Mary, Illustrator. *The Tempest,* by William Shakespeare. Published by Grabhorn Press, San Francisco, 1951.

Grabhorn, Mary, Illustrator. *The Tragedie of Macbeth,* by William Shakespeare. Published by Grabhorn Press, San Francisco, 1952.

Grabhorn, Mary, Illustrator. *The Tragedy of Richard III,* by William Shakespeare. Published by Grabhorn Press, San Francisco, 1953.

Grabhorn, Mary, Illustrator. *A Midsommer Nights Dreame,* by William Shakespeare. Published by Grabhorn Press, San Francisco, 1955.

Gromaire, Marcel, Illustrator. *Macbeth,* by William Shakespeare. Published in Paris, 1958.

Nevelson, Louise, Illustrator. *Orfeo and Euridice*. Music by Christoph W. Gluck, libretto by Raniero de Calzabigi. Published in St. Louis, 1984.

PAINTINGS, WATERCOLORS AND DRAWINGS

Derain, André
Illustrations for Oscar Wilde's *Salomé*, 1938. Watercolor, gouache and ink.
"Two Soldiers," 11¾ x 9".
"Four Jews," 8½ x 9⅝".
"Herodias," 10½ x 9¼".
Illustrated on page 9.
"Guard," 8½ x 9".
"Salomé and Herod Antipas," 11½ x 9½".
"Salomé and Herodias," 9½ x 9½".
"Iokanaan, the Prophet," 12 x 9".
Illustrated on page 19.
"Salomé and Soldier," 10½ x 9⅜".
"Salomé Dancing," 9 x 9½".
"Naaman, the Executioner," 10 x 9".
"Salomé and a Slave," 10 x 9¼".
"Salomé Speaking to the Beheaded Iokanaan," 10½ x 9¼".
"Salomé Beheaded," 8½ x 9½".

Craig, Edward Gordon
"Hamlet Decor," 1905. Watercolor, crayon, ink and chalk, 21 x 17'.'
Illustrated on page 12.
"Battle Scene from Hamlet," 1926. Watercolor, crayon and gouache, 10⅜ x 10½".

Mielziner, Jo
Five scenes from *Salomé*, 1921. Ink and crayon.
Scene 1, 2½ x 3½". (Upper left)
Scene 2, 2½ x 3½". (Upper right)
Scene 3, 2½ x 3⅝". (Lower left)
Scene 4, 2½ x 3½". (Lower right)
Scene 5, 3 x 4½". (Center)

Cocteau, Jean
"Untitled" (Head), n.d. Ink, 8 x 10", variable.
"Two heads in Profile," 1938. Pencil, colored pencil and ball point pen, 7¾ x 4½", variable.
"Portrait of Jean Marais," 1938. Pencil, 9½ x 6⅛", variable.

Moiseiwitsch, Tanya
Costume design for *Richard III*, 1953. Watercolor, gouache and ink.
"Queen Elizabeth," 13⅜ x 10¾".
Costume designs for *Antony and Cleopatra*, 1967. Watercolor, gouache and ink.
"Charmain," 13¾ x 10".
"Antony," 13⅞ x 9⅞".

Healy, Desmond
Costume designs for *Hamlet*, 1957. Watercolor, gouache and pencil.

"Bernardo and Francesco," 12 x 7½".
"Lords of the Council," 12 x 7¼.".
"A Player," 12 x 7½".
"Court Lady," 12 x 7½".
"Duel Scene," 12 x 7½".
"Gertrude," 12 x 7½".
Costume designs for *Richard III*, 1967. Ink and gouache.
"Richard III," 13¼ x 8⅛".
"Lady Anne," 13½ x 8".
Morris, George Lovett Kingsland
"Requiem for the Met. #2," 1967. Oil on canvas, 44⅜ x 53". **Cover Illustration.**

Israel, Robert
Costumes and scene designs from *Akhnaton*, 1983. Watercolor and felt-tip pen.
(All sizes are variable.)
1. "Eight Fighting Men," 25 x 16½".
2,3. "Harvester and Bricklayer," 24 x 17". Not in exhibition.
4. "Harvester," 23 x 17".
5. "Amon Priests," 25 x 17".
6. "Head Amon Priest," 25½ x 17½".
7. "Amenhotep III," 25½ x 16".
8. "God in Human Form," 25½ x 17½".
9. "Ram/Khnum and Hawk/Horus Gods—Four Canopic Jars," 24 x 18½". **Illustrated on page 21.**
10. "Hapi Thoth/Ape and Ibis Gods," 24½ x 18".
11. "Seth Hathor/Aardvark and Bull Gods," 25½ x 18½".
12. "Anubus Jackal God," 24½ x 16½".
13. "Aye at the Funeral of Amenhotep III," 24¼ x 16½". Not in exhibition.
14A. "Akhnaton Nude," 25 x 17". Not in exhibition.
14. "Akhnaton at Funeral of Amenhotep III," 24¾ x 16".
15. "Nefertiti at Funeral of Amenhotep III," 24½ x 17".
16,20,23. "Tye in Act II Costume," 27 x 17½".
17. "Horemhab in Coronation Gown," 24¼ x 16½".
18. "Akhnaton in Coronation Gown with Crown," 28 x 20".
19. "Nefertiti in Coronation Gown," 26½ x 18". **Illustrated on page 15.**
21. "Akhnaton in Hymn Costume," 24½ x 14½". Not in exhibition.
22. "Nefertiti in Act II Costume," 27½ x 17".
24. "Antonist Priests," 25½ x 17".
25. "Horemhab as General," 26 x 16¼".
26. "Three Female Slaves," 25½ x 17". Not in exhibition.
27. "Male Slave," 24¼ x 15½". Not in exhibition.
28. "Six Daughters—Variations," 24½ x 16".
29. "Aye in Act III," 24 x 17".
30. "Tour Guide," 26 x 17".
31. "Tourist", 23½ x 17½". Not in exhibition.
32. "Three Tourists," 24½ x 17½".
33. "Tourist," 24 x 14½".

34. "Tourist," 25½ x 17½".
    Not in exhibition.
35. "Three Tourists," 25 x 17½".
    Not in exhibition.
36. "Tourist," 24½ x 15½".
    Not in exhibition.
37. "Tourist," 26 x 17".
38. "Tourist," 24¼ x 16".
39. "Male Chorus—Draw String
    Waist/Collar . . .," 24¼ x 18¼".
    Not in exhibition.
40. "Female Chorus—Draw String Waist
    Pajamas," 23 x 18".
41. "Column," 24½ x 13". Not in exhibition.
42. "Column," 26 x 12". Not in exhibition.
43. "Temple of Transitions," 22¼ x 17¼".
44. "Forty-Five Gold Leafed Totems from 4'
    to 7'," 15 x 26". Not in exhibition.

Nevelson, Louise
    Illustrations for *Orfeo and Euridice: An Opera
    in One Act*, 1984.
    Watercolor, ink, and pencil.
    Scene I, 12¼ x 9⅛".
    Scene II, 12¼ x 9⅛".
    Scene III, 12⅜ x 9¼".
    Scene IV, 12¼ x 10¼".
    Scene IV, 12⅜ x 18¼".
    Scene V, 12¼ x 9¼".
    Scene V, 12⅛ x 9⅛".

PRINTS

Torelli, Giacomo
    Engravings from *Il Bellerofonte*, 1642.
    "Harbor in Patera, Venice." Prologue.
    Engraving, 9⅜ x 12⅜".
    Illustrated on page 17.
    "Harbor in Patera." Act I, scenes 1-3.
    Engraving, 9⅜ x 12⅜".
    "Cave of the Winds." Act I, scene 2.
    Engraving, 9⅜ x 12⅜".
    Illustrated on page 6.
    "Palace Courtyard." Act I, scenes 4-10.
    Engraving, 9⅜ x 12⅜".
    "Desert Island." Act II, scene 2. Engraving,
    9⅜ x 12⅜".
    "Deserted Island, Venus' Temple in the
    Sky." Act II, scene 3. Engraving, 9⅜ x 12⅜".
    "Jupiter's Temple." Act II, scene 11.
    Engraving, 9⅜ x 12⅜".
    "A Garden in Venice." Act II, scenes 4-10.
    Engraving, 9⅜ x 12⅜".
    "Palace Garden." Act III, scenes 1-7.
    Engraving, 9⅜ x 12⅜".
    "Palace Chamber." Act III, scenes 8-12.
    Engraving, 9⅜ x 12⅜".

Delacroix, Eugène
    Lithographs from *Hamlet*, 1843. (The 1954
    Folio Society Edition of Shakespeare's
    Hamlet was consulted for the English text.)
    "Good Hamlet . . ." Act I, scene 2.
    Lithograph, 10 x 7⅞".
    "My fate cries out . . ." Act I, scene 4.

Lithograph, 10⅛ x 8".
    "I am your father's ghost." Act I, scene 5.
    Lithograph, 10⅛ x 7⅝".
    "What are you reading, sir?" Act II, scene 2.
    Lithograph, 9¾ x 7⅛".
    "It's a villanous intrigue . . ." Act III,
    scene 2. Lithograph, 9¾ x 12¾"
    "Will you play upon this pipe?" Act III,
    scene 2. Lithograph, 10 x 8". Not in
    exhibition.
    "I could easily kill him now . . ." Act III,
    scene 3. Lithograph, 10⅜ x 7⅛".
    Not in exhibition.
    "How now, a rat!" Act III, scene 4.
    Lithograph, 9½ x 7⅝". Not in exhibition.
    "This counselor is now most still, most
    secret . . ." Act III, scene 4. Lithograph,
    10 x 7". Not in exhibition.
    "Add nothing more . . ." Act IV, scene 5.
    Lithograph, 10⅛ x 7".
    " . . . her garments, heavy with their drink,
    pulled the poor wretch . . ." Act IV,
    scene 7. Lithograph, 7¼ x 10".
    Illustrated on page 18.
    "This skull, Sir, was that of Yorrick, the
    King's jester." Act V, scene 1. Lithograph,
    11⅛ x 8⅜". **Illustrated on page 11.**
    "Oh, I die, Horatio . . ." Act V, scene 2.
    Lithograph, 11¼ x 8".

Craig, Edward Gordon
    Hamlet, 1930
    "Costume design for Hamlet." Woodcut,
    6½ x 2½".
    "Costume design for Rosencrantz and
    Guildenstern." Woodcut, 5½ x 3¼".

Lindner, Richard
    "Der Rosenkavalier," n.d. Color lithograph,
    28⅜ x 21".

OBJECTS

Senn, Herbert and Pond, Helen.
    Maquette for *Der Rosenkavalier*, 1981.
    Watercolor and gouache, 4¾ x 8¼ x 3¼".

Nevelson, Louise
    Necklace worn by special guests for the
    opening night of *Orfeo and Euridice*, 1984.
    Aluminum, gold leaf, ink and silk string,
    6½ x 4", variable.

ILLUSTRATION INDEX

Designed by Jerry Tokola
Design, typesetting, and printing by Best Printing Company
Bound by Custom Bookbinders
Photography by Michael Smith